Sundays in Camp
James Black DD

"Drill your units until conscious effort glides into instinct, but remember that a thousand soldiers are a thousand souls"

Parvus Magna Press

5 Ambleside Close, Leyton, London, E10 5RU

Email: sic@pmpress.co.uk

Website: www.pmpress.co.uk

James Blacks' awesome book Around the Guns is now public domain so we could not bring ourselves to copyright this edition.

If you like this edition and you have an idea of another you would like to see please let us know!!

British Library Cataloguing in Publication Data

A catalogue record and a copy of this book are available from the British Library

ISBN 978-1-910372-10-4 **Paperback**
ISBN 978-1-910372-11-1 **Paperback**
ISBN 978-1-910372-12-8 **eBook**

Parvus Magna Press publishes limited run and niche interest books in the UK. If you would like to see your book in print, please email your manuscript to sic@pmpress.co.uk

The Evangelical Heritage Library

Welcome to the Evangelical Heritage Library.

There are some books whose impact on the lives of successive generations of Christians deserve to be preserved and distributed as widely as possible.

When I was first approached to edit the Evangelical Heritage Library, I knew for sure the books I wanted to see included and was pleasantly surprised to see them all there on the list.

Some of the books on our list have been out of print for over 100 years and although the odd volume can be found here and there in second hand shops they are mostly lost to the wider public.

The Evangelical Heritage Library format is intended to encourage the reader to study the subjects alongside the author, to this end we have added a couple of extra's to the format of the books.

Wide Outer Margin – we have added the wide margin to allow the reader to mark up and annotate their volume with ease. I have found the issue with studying with antiquated books is that it is close to sacrilege to mark their ancient pages.

We have added, where necessary, footnotes to explain obsolete or archaic text and to give context to references that may be unfamiliar.

It is our fervent prayer that this library provides you a route to the throne of God, that there, before His throne, you will get to know Him and the power of His love.

About the Author

James Black, born 1826 Berwickshire and started his public pulpit ministry in 1854. He was a leading light in the United Presbyterian Church and the United Reform church throughout his ministry.

Apart from this excellent book Around the Guns, James black is also the author of The Mystery of Preaching which is also available in the Evangelical Heritage Library.

The Unlocked Door and The Christian Life are both excellent reads and recommended to the reader without reservation.

I first came across the title Around The Guns about 15 years ago in a reference from another work (whose title has slipped my mind) – however as the years have rolled by I had almost given up hope of finding my own copy.

Imagine my immense pleasure when I found a copy in a friend's library and he allowed me to borrow it! My first thought was to make this tome available to all who would search forever – so here it is.

James Black manages to communicate the gospel with a clarity and fervour that are infectious and although his illustrations and stories may seem at first to be dated and without application in this modern computerised world, the underlying message comes through loud and clear.

I enjoyed transcribing this book thoroughly and more than once found my prayer closet to deal with issues in my own heart that I felt I had already dealt with years ago.

I hope this volume blesses you and your ministry just as it has blessed mine.

Sharif George

Parvus Magna Press 2016

Foreword

My three months with our troops at the Forth Defences were a pure joy – thanks largely to the unfailing kindness and courtesy of the offices and the men with whom I served. In preparing these talks at the suggestion of some friends, I have re-lived much of the past happiness, for I see before me the faces of many whom I now count comrades. To them, too many to name – good fellow all, keen soldiers, fine men – may I take the liberty of inscribing this book?

The title is true. Not a few of these talks, in the April and May sunshine with which we were favoured, were given round the gun-platforms of the various batteries.

To the officers and men of the 4th R.G.A., the Royal Engineers (Edinburgh company), and the various infantry battalions which stayed with us for a little on their road to the Front, I desire to express my thanks and remembrance.

J.B.

Contents

With The Pipers To Church

TRAMP! Tramp! to the skirl of the pipes. It was a joy to swing along the road with you to service this morning, the sunshine around us, and the green-tipped hedges announcing that summer is near. The quaint lines of the "Ancient Mariner" stole into my mind: —

"O sweeter than the marriage-feast,
'Tis sweeter far to me,
To walk together to the kirk
With a goodly company!"

Why did you come to church parade? I see you smile at my artless question, and I fancy I can overhear your answer. "Battalion orders, Sir! We come here—because we must!"

That may be so; but may I say that if you come here only from duty you will be little the better

of it? Forced service generally goes against the grain. I can well believe that a man may

attend this service under the compulsion of battalion orders and may yet find some good in it; but speaking for myself, I should feel more ease in addressing you, if I knew that you came for a better reason. I should like, therefore, to point out to you in what spirit and for what purpose we should attend a service such as this.

May I introduce what I have to say by an anecdote? There was a minister in a neighbouring city who was reputed to have a happy knack in addressing children, and as a result of his interest the young people responded very well to his attentions. One young girl in his congregation had accompanied her mother to a "high-art" concert, and of course, as with one of her age, had been openly bored! On the way home she asked her mother what the concert had cost, and on learning the price replied, "What a sum to pay for a performance that only made me sleepy! Whereas if we go to church, we can give what we like in the offering and get more fun."

Fun at a church service! If the average young person were frank, he would admit that the

ordinary church service is a trial to his soul. It is refreshing, therefore, to hear of someone who goes to church for fun, for some special interest and appeal in the service. And yet this is no new or unnatural idea. An old psalmist once expressed the same thought in other words:

"I was glad when they said unto me, Let us go into the house of the Lord." -

Glad to go to church! Have we not imagined church-going to be a duty rather than a pleasure? I can remember when a lad how a long church service was a strain on my small stock of patience. I found the minister sleepy, the atmosphere sleepy, and myself sleepy; and, unfortunately, just when I was ready to drop off into a blessed forgetfulness there was always an inconvenient parent at hand to jog me into wakefulness. I used to vow that when I grew up I would give the church a wide berth.

And yet, here am I to-day, a minister and chaplain, asking your interest in this service. What is the reason of my change of front? Simply this—that, like the little girl, I have learned to regard the church with joy I as soon as I began to understand what the church stood for, and to know something of the gracious Lord whom it represented, the thought of it filled my heart with gladness. Fellow-soldiers, why should we not have joy in coming to church If we thought of all the goodness God bestows on us every day of our lives, if we remembered that all we have is the gift of His love, if we looked about this beautiful world and said, "All this is a token of our Father," if we considered His redeeming love in Jesus our Lord, if we thought of the forgiveness, the peace, and the promise made ours in Christ, why! our hearts would be so full of thankfulness that we would go up to God's house with a high joy to praise Him for His goodness! Why do we not?

Listen! To think is to thank. The secret lies there. It is because you and I do not think that we are so ungrateful. We take everything for granted, as if it were a matter of course, and in consequence the God of our life remains unremembered. Think for a moment of all the mercy and goodness of God. Cast your eyes round this wonderful world. Look into the mystery of your own dreaming soul. Then I am sure you will be ready to cry with a new understanding, "I was glad when they said unto me let us go into the house of the Lord."

Another object we should have in this service is fellowship. We come here because we desire to have fellowship or communion with one another and with God. I wonder if you realise that united worship such as this has a special blessing. Did not our Lord once say, "Where two or three are gathered together in My name, there am I in the midst of them." Try to realise this – because you are here, He is here!

Be very still and very worshipful, for in coming here to-day you brought your Lord with you! That is why we expect to have fellowship, because God is truly a person, one who is ready to be a friend. How friendly He is you can only understand when you think of Him as seen in Jesus, one who has a great love for your welfare, who is grieved when you hurt your own soul with sin, who is anxious each hour to keep you from falling, and who longs to lead you into life's true happiness. You know what a great thing it is to have fellowship with a good friend. I have watched some of you walking along the road and opening your heart to some friend or companion. I trust you all know the value and comfort of a true friend; you need one here amid the increased temptation of camp life. And yet, I tell you, men, you have no friend on earth who has your welfare so much at heart as Jesus, the friend of men. If you would only let yourself know Him, and get into a real companionship with Him, His influence would be the best thing in your life. Think of what a true friend can do—cheer you, strengthen you, help you when you are down, and be a sort of "other part" of yourself. May I commend Jesus to you now as the true friend of your soul? His friendship will lead you to everything that is good and beautiful, and will save you from the snares of your own heart. If only we could begin to form that strong bond now, it would be our salvation.

A third reason for this church parade is food. I began by asking why we come here at all. A part, and a big part, of the answer lies in this that we feel our souls are hungry and need food.

I have been amused to notice how lively the men are at "ration time" when the bugle sounds "Come to the cook-house door!" The tang of the sea air at Queensferry gives a fine edge to our appetite, which has its complementary side in the tanned faces and robust health in which we all exult. Try to run a battalion for a day without food, and you may expect a mutiny. We recognise that these bodies of ours need food, good and sufficient, if we are to do the work of men. It has been said that a soldier fights on his stomach. Many campaigns have been won or lost in their commissariat.

This applies also to the mind, a truth we all admit. We cannot train and educate our minds unless we give them the food they need—books, thought, study, and mental exercise. These things feed the mind; it lives or starves by what it gets.

Is it not remarkable that while we recognise the needs of our body and mind, we seem to forget that our spiritual nature is fed and nourished in the same way? Crowds of young people imagine that they can grow good by chance! How casual and how careless is our training of our soul—a chance attendance at church, an occasional reading of the Bible, and an even more occasional prayer. I tell you, men, if your body cannot live without food, neither can your soul. It will die like a wilted flower.

If there is anything eternal in us, it is our spiritual nature. We are what our soul is. It would be folly on our part to make ourselves fine animals, or even fine minds, if we did not also make ourselves fine souls. We are placed in this world by God to become men—men in the deepest sense, with character and life developed and enriched as God would have them. No matter how rich or talented or learned a man is, he is a poor being, in the eyes of man and God if he has not grown a soul. We feel that whatever we are or are not, we are spiritual beings with a spiritual destiny. How am I to face God if I have starved my soul?

We come then to this service for food, to build up our spiritual life as we build up muscle in our bodies. In the offering of praise, in the giving of thanks, in the prayers of confession and aspiration, in the fellowship with one another and with God, in the reading and preaching of the Word, there lie the germs of our soul's life. I urge you to be diligent in the use of your opportunities. Take your New Testament (I know you all have a copy), and get to know and love Him whose life is the source of all true life. Open your hearts now and then in prayer. It need not be a formal business. As you walk along the road and see the sky above you and the flowers at your feet, murmur some broken thanks to God. In any hour of trial ask His strength. In your quiet moments meditate a little on God's goodness and glory. That is prayer. So by study and meditation, give your soul its food.

After what I have said, I trust that none of us will ever say again that we come to this service by battalion orders. Come only by the "order" of your desire and need. Come not because you must but because you may. Come to praise your Redeemer. Come to get strength for tomorrow's temptations that you may be able on all occasions to play the man. Come because your heart is full, and because you need God to make your life perfect. Next Sunday, as you march from your various billets, interpret the skirl of the pipes after this fashion:

*"I was glad when they said unto me,
Let us go into the house of the Lord."*

When Knights Were Bold

THE world has always had its fighters, but how different they have been in every age! You gunners who stand duty beside your big "barkers" and you men of the line who handle your rifles Would be inclined to smile if you were pitted against some of the warriors of ancient days.

Suppose, as We left church this morning, there came down the road mounted on a prancing steed, a knight of the olden days How you would smile as he unloosed his lance, set it in position, and charged down on you in his jingling armour. Any one of you who has been practising at the range could "pick him off" before he was Within shouting distance. Truly, different times have different manners; and the knight of old, clad alike in steel and stilted language, seems to us more comic than heroic, a relic of the past, like the perfume of old lavender.

Yet, while we smile tolerantly at his methods and his weapons, it would be foolish to smile at him. He was the finest product of a fine idealism. There may have been bad knights, just as there are bad soldiers to-day; but the institution of knighthood itself was one of the big dreams of man's chivalrous soul. It stood for something good and gracious in Europe's dark days.

Is the day of chivalry past, when men went out to do deeds of daring on behalf of the weak and the oppressed? The knight may have gone, like a broken antique into the lumber-room, but knighthood and chivalry have remained. For so long as we have brave soldiers and sailors who sacrifice their lives for others, who go to their death on behalf of the oppressed, and who act honourably and courteously to their friends and foes alike, we may be proud of our modern knights.

I should like you this morning to learn some lessons from the life of the days "when knights were bold." I am sure there are certain qualities in the Warriors of olden days which, if you could imitate them, would make you better and more efficient soldiers in your own day ot crisis.

In the first place, I should like to describe to you, in somewhat haphazard fashion, a few of the rites which the young knight had to undergo before he became a full soldier, an accredited man-of-arms.

To begin with, knighthood was an institution of the Church, and the young warrior professed himself a servant of God. Look, for instance, at the striking ceremony through which he had to pass. When a young man had finished his practice in arms, such as you are now undergoing, learning his weapons and the rules of warfare, he received the blessing of the Church. To obtain this, he was taken to some chapel at night-fall, and was left there alone throughout the eerie darkness. Some of you may have seen a famous picture of such an incident, where the young man, clad in armour, is shown to be kneeling in prayer before the altar. In front of him, on the altar, are laid his sword and lance, and a piece of his armour.

What was this meant to suggest? In the first place, I understand that by this rite he was consecrating himself and his sword for God. Power, let us remember, may be a blessing or a curse. What a terrible scourge is a wild, un-consecrated sword! All the horrors and cruelties of war spring from a selfish and evil use of power. On the other hand, there is such a thing as a sword "bathed in heaven" a sword that is drawn only to uphold right and punish wrong, used for the king on earth and the King in heaven. I Wonder, for instance, what our colonel would say if I asked him to baptise our guns! Do not smile at my remark. There is a sense, as with the ancient knights, in which these roaring guns of yours may be baptised for the service of goodness and truth. God grant that we in Britain always go to war only for righteousness and justice. Let us lay our rifles on the altar of God, and vow that we shall use them only for truth and liberty.

But again, by his act, the young knight was acknowledging that there should be a religious basis underlying his warfare. He was a servant of the king; but, as an old worthy once said, "There are two kings in Scotland." We serve King George, but we also serve King Christ: and I fully believe that the man who most truly serves King Christ will be the best subject of King George. Religion always manufactures the finest citizens, for it is the one basis for an upright, clean, straight, and godly life. I shall even go so far as to say that the best soldiers are always Christian men. Ask yourselves this – Who were the finest soldiers England and Scotland ever produced? Without any doubt England's stoutest warriors were Cromwell's Puritans, well called "Ironsides," men who fought from conscience and a passion for justice. How they made Europe quake! And as surely our finest fighters in Scotland were the men of the Reformation and the Covenant, who by their valour made Scotland what it is to-day. My fellow-soldiers, what We need to carry us through these tragic times is a religious basis in our warfare. After all, it is a mere incident that we are fighting Germany: the main thing is that we have taken up arms for Belgium, for the oppressed, for truth, for justice, for God... Let us only get some passion for righteousness in our hearts, and We shall be the better soldiers for it. There is nothing to strengthen a man's arms like a love of honour and a hatred of Wrong. An officer in the regular Army once said to me that his men in India were just "pagan devils, and by Jove they could fight." But there is no endurance and no desperation like the endurance and desperation of a good man. Good will always conquer evil in the long run, because however "devils" may fight, "angels" can fight better. Get a passion for God into your blood, my men, and you will be the better soldiers for it!

' But further, after the night vigil in the chapel, the young Warrior came forth at the break of dawn, and another symbolic service took place. An old and tried knight stepped forward with three coloured robes on his arm. Advancing to the young soldier, he first robed him in a white garment, then in a red garment, and last in a black garment. What was the idea underlying this quaint rite? If you think of it, you will agree that in its symbolic meaning it was a beautiful ceremony.

The White robe! Why, what signifies purity and honour more than this? Tennyson speaks of the "white flower of a blameless life." In putting on the white robe the young man was silently promising to lead a pure, just and honourable life. Do you think, my fellow-soldiers, that you could put on that white robe of honour? It would make you better men and finer soldiers.

The red robe! That meant the red blood of Christ which had been poured out for men. By this the aspiring knight was vowing that he would give his blood for Christ, who had given His blood for him. To stand by Christ's Kingdom, to further the interests of righteousness and truth, to see that the weak and the oppressed are honoured and righted, what could be more fitting for a young soldier to promise? Could you promise that? If you could, it would make you finer warriors.

The black robe! Need I explain that?

Yesterday I attended the funeral of one of your comrades, and I put the black band on my left arm. The dark robe of the knight was life's remembrancer of death. This is a matter we all do Well to remember. Youth may be a fierce and wild thing. It is conscious of its pulsing blood and its hot passions. It feels as if

17

there was nothing it could not do. Life is at its feet, and it is apt to treat life as if it were at its feet. My comrades, let us remember that our life is short, and at the end there is a Holy Judge, Be chary of wasted hours, and unused talents, and youth's unreasoning spendthrift ways. I would not Wish you for a moment to darken your long spring days with unseasonable thoughts of autumn. But, death is a thing that every man-of-arms must be ready to face—God knows how soon! But let it come soon or late, the man who fears God need never fear death. Christ has conquered death, and in Christ eternal life is yours. The black robe! Let it be a reminder not of death, but of life—the full rich life of the Christian. With that death does not matter.

Had time allowed I should have liked to speak to you of the vows which the young knight took on his lips. In their spirit they would have done honour to any man among us. May I summarise them in the following sentences: —

I vow to honour God.
I vow to honour law.
I vow to honour man.
I vow to honour woman.
I vow to honour myself.

A great programme, surely, for a warrior, ancient or modern! I shall close by remarking only on two of these vows. In the first instance, what about honouring women, young soldiers? Shame on any man who misuses the nation's sentimentality towards the khaki, and holds his own or another's honour lightly. Sin not against the home from which you come, and the home you may sometime hope to have! Listen to me, gentlemen of the King!

And, lastly, what about honouring yourselves? Honour these bodies of yours against all excess. I Wish the nation had taken some timely care for the increased temptations of your camp life. In the absence of this, it is only the more laid on you to take care of yourselves, and, above all, to take care of weaker comrades.

I bid you good-morning, knights of the King.

White Magic

THE scene is a small grey chamber, lighted by flickering candles and a low steady fire. On the fire, or adjoining it, are varied pots and crucibles, and hovering over the pots, watching and stirring them, is an old man, curiously arrayed in a flowing robe that evidently, like its owner, has seen better days. But for his eyes, which rival the fire in their glint, one would say that he is bowed by years and trouble. Watch him as his feverish eyes flash over his pots. Now and then he practises strange movements, and his lips mutter weird incantations. At times he breaks out into little snatches of exultation, broken again by deep sighs. At last, after some final rites, he lifts the pots and lays them aside to cool. Then, having examined his results with trembling anxiety, he utters a low moan and drops like a broken thing on the floor. "Who can bring gold out of lead? Not one!"

Another scene. This time a man as broken and as heavy with trouble. For years he has been trying the same miracle, but in a different sphere. The lead in his case is the rough alloy of his own poor human nature; the gold he longs for is the pure and upright heart. Vainly, like the alchemist, he has tried to transmute the one into the other. But at length, broken with his trouble, he too bows before the impossible. "Who can bring the clean out of the unclean? Not one!"

Not one! Is that the verdict? If so, life and all our strivings are streaked with tragedy.

One! That is the verdict. For Christ has done the impossible. He is the Alchemist of life: and by His strange white magic He has converted the lead into gold, the unclean into the clean. "He is able to save them to the uttermost that come unto God by Him."

Christ has done it. We do not say merely that He can do it; we say that He has done it, and is doing it to-day. He was always a Worker of miracles; but He worked none more astounding than this—gold out of lead, the clean out of the unclean.

Look at the men of His own day. I see first an extortioner, a man as fond of the world's gear, and as close—fisted and dishonest in acquiring it, as any shady company promoter of our own time. This man, in order to make money, has turned against his own people and has farmed out taxes for the hated Roman.

How has he done it--by subtle rogueries--his own confession tells. Yet when Christ comes into touch with this man, His influence so works on his hard heart that the miracle is Wrought. And so Zacchaeus stands up and cries, "The half of my goods I give to the poor; and if I have taken anything from any man by false accusation, I restore him fourfold." It is the work of the Magician, lead into gold, the unclean into the clean.

I see another, one of earth's waifs, the saddest thing in God's world, a woman of the streets. See how the people draw in their skirts, lest by chance they should touch her in passing. She has lowered her Womanhood in the dust, and the dust has soiled her like the plague. The Magdalene—has not that name become a byword? Who can restore her virtue and cleanse her vicious life? "Who can bring the clean out of the unclean? Not one!" Yes, One! For when the Purifying touch of Jesus is laid on her life, she forsakes her past ways like a worn-out garment, and the Magdalene washes the Magician's feet with her tears, tears that wash two things, His feet and her heart. White Magic, I say – lead into gold!

The magic has gone on; it has been the same down the centuries. Wherever Christ has gone He has done the impossible. Why baulk at His miracles? What is it to cure a paralytic compared with curing a moral twist? There is a disease of the soul that is worse than any disease of the limbs; and at this moment there are thousands of men who are living testimonies of His magic power over the soul. He has done it; and He is doing it now.

But this is old—fashioned; the day of the gospel is past. Men still want to bring the gold out of lead, but they want it in a more modern style. What suited yesterday, with its unscientific views, will not suit to—day. We need white magic, but the day of the old magician is gone.

I look around on the modern efforts of men to achieve the old miracle. "Who can bring gold out of lead?" There steps forward one with a new scheme and doctrine, which will give new worlds for old, changing the unclean into the clean. I hear him advocate the clearing of our slums, the better housing of our struggling workers, more light, more air, and more leisure. I listen to worthy talks about the redistribution of wealth, a fairer chance for the children, and a general elevation of the masses through cleanliness, health, and comfort. Nothing could be better, and certainly nothing is more needed. There are people trying to lead lives where a true life is scarcely possible. I know it all, and my heart is sore. But are bread and comfort the be-all and the end-all? Will any mere change of social conditions work the old miracle and bring in the age of gold? My comrades, we want the clean out of the unclean, but, in my experience, you may put a pig in a palace, but unless you first change the heart of the pig, all that will be changed is the palace. Gold out of lead! Is it not here that our modern alchemist fails?

Another steps forward, with a scheme that seems more promising. Ignorance, he says, is the root of sin. What the world needs is a true and deep knowledge. Men are what they are because they do not know any better. Make education more general; teach men and women truth and knowledge, and the day of miracles will arrive. If men know what is right they will do it, for all sin is ignorance. It sounds modern and convincing, but it is as old as the day of Socrates. And it is condemned by this—that from the day of Socrates it has been futile. For often, as we are unfortunately learning in this ghastly war, knowledge and science only refine and perfect the means of sin and cruelty. Moreover, here is the conclusion of the whole matter. Tell me if, when you sinned to-day, you did not do it against knowledge and light and leading. "Who can bring gold out of lead? Not one!"

I see another, who proclaims the way to the great miracle, a strong, virile, eager man. I like his doctrine, for there is a great truth in its depths. "Will," he says, "is the way to the miracle." We must put resolution and backbone into our people, for the only thing that can lift a man is his own will. Iron, brethren, iron in our hearts! We must teach men to shut their teeth and clench their hands, and so win through. That way lies the miracle, the clean out of the unclean. But however true this is, does our friend not forget that 'will' is the root of all sin as well as of all good? Is there not such a thing as the will to sin? Moreover, here is a final problem—the men we want and need to save are precisely those who have no will. How can a man make up his mind when he has no mind to make up? The first thing you have to do is to put a will into him; and where are you to get it? "Who can bring gold out of lead? Not one!"

And, lastly, here is a suave and easy-going fellow who points to the coming day of miracles, Evolution is the secret of it all. The world is gradually evolving a better and finer type of man, and in time we shall naturally accomplish the impossible. Sometime hence (God knows how long!) there will people this earth a race of men and women, naturally evolved by the processes of life, who will reach the great ideal, the age of gold. Well, I can dream with any one; but I am not going to dream such a folly as the myth that evolution necessarily means progress. It doesn't; it often means degeneration. Moreover, am I not entitled to inquire how, in all conscience, this age—long process is going to help me? I Want the miracle performed in me, and I shall be dust in a few short years. Comrades, I think you can settle this theorist by one pertinent inquiry. How is all this long progress going to help the man in the gutter? "Who can bring gold out of lead? Not one!"

So much for the modern theories which have tickled your minds. When put to the touchstone, what do they offer you? I offer you today the proved thing, a method that has never failed with any who have given it a chance. The Lord Jesus can change a man's heart; and, if He had the chance, He would change the World's heart. I hear some men speak lightly of the failure of Christianity. It has never failed, except Where it has failed to be failed to be accepted. Twenty centuries of Christianity, and is this all? This day of red ruin, this forgetfulness of God and humanity, Europe again in the savage age; and after twenty centuries! No, a thousand times No! Christianity has never been accepted through these long centuries. We have run our commerce, our politics, our social relations, and our diplomacy without any reference to the Word and Cross of Christ. Christianity has not failed, for the simple reason that it has not been tried. Let Europe give it a trial to-day, and see the difference. Let love and gentleness and sacrifice be the mottoes of national and international life, and the world would be startled by the results. A fool's dream, you say. Trade and diplomacy cannot be run on such lines. Perhaps not, certainly not as they are at present. But do not blame Christianity for having failed where it has never been tried. The nations are bleeding to-day because they have forgotten that Christ once bled.

Where He is accepted Christ works the great miracle of the Alchemist. Changed lives tell their own tale. Have you no desire for this White magic that brings gold out of lead, and the clean out of the unclean? Someday, if you neglect this offer, you will cry like Job, "Who can bring the clean out of the unclean, the good out of evil, hope out of despair, life out of death? Not one!" – Yes, One!

Three Men In A Block-House

Three men in a block-house chatting with the padre. After some talk one of the men remarks, "All I say is, I don't know What good the Church is going to do me."

That is a blunt statement. We live in a practical age, when men have learned to test a thing by What it is worth. We have a right to ask What the Church has to offer us. I prefer that a man should take such an attitude than that he should come here indifferently.

What has Christ to offer you for the living of your life? I could mention many things, but I shall confine myself to three points. And I hold regarding them that these three things are necessary for the living of a full life; and, further, that Jesus Christ can alone give them. That is a big statement, but I hope to uphold it.

In the first place, I believe that every man before me needs and desires a new start. I do not know your life, but I know my own; and as I look back upon my own past, I admit that there are things I would gladly blot out if I could. However uprightly a man may have lived, he has no reason to be content with. what he has done or been. Each one of us, if he is honest with himself, must confess this. Our past is full of follies, indiscretions, mistakes, and sins, would that we could cry:

"Old past, let go and drop in the sea
Till fathomless waters cover thee."

But there it is facing us, and if we are wise, we shall turn and face it.

Who is going to give us this fresh start? Men cannot forgive us, for it is not only against men we have sinned. It does not do to forget; the thing is there in spite of all we can do, and will one day face us. Some of us have gone to varied sources—to thinkers, and books, and systems but we have discovered in bitterness of heart that none of these can touch our problem or give us the peace we desire.

If Jesus came to give us any gift it was the gift of forgiveness. His message centred round the love and grace of God. He spoke of the infinite tenderness of our Father who so loves His erring children that He is ready to receive all who come to Him in repentance. This is a great truth to which thousands of Christians have borne testimony—men and women who in the strength of Christ have conquered not only sin but even the desire of it. They have been lifted out of themselves. They have had the load eased from their shoulders. They have received the gift of a new start.

Another thing which every man both needs and desires is daily guidance. Our life is full of traps and snares to catch the unwary, and even the best of us requires a helping hand. I sometimes wish that life's roads had plain sign-posts telling where each bye—path leads; but instead of that, we have to blunder on into each until we are brought up by a hedge of thorns. We sin so often through ignorance, and it is only the sting and bitterness that open our eyes. I seldom go into a chemist's shop without wishing that life could be labelled out like his bottles: "Poison."   Most of our young people only discover the poison too late.

I believe that in this life, with all its moral puzzles, the greatest good a man could receive would be the gift of a straight road or a friend to guide him at the turns. Who does not know the tragedy of the wrong turn? Once taken, it is so difficult to correct. Once committed to it we are so stubborn to admit our folly. If I know my heart, I would say that the great need of every man before me is just the need of daily guidance amid life's problems.

I proclaim Jesus to you as life's guide. "He died that He might bring us to God." He lived our life that We in turn might know how to live like Him. He tasted our temptations that by His strength and experience We might bear ours like men. And, in addition to His example, He has given us His law and teaching to guide us amid our perplexities, laws so plain that even a wayfaring man need not err therein.

I once had the happiness of spending a spring vacation in Holland when the fields of tulips dazzled the eyes like diamonds. By the goodness of a friend I received an invitation to visit one of the bulb farms round Haarlem, and with my Wife and friends I proceeded there one day to see the tulips. As you may know, Holland is a flat sandy plain, made fertile by innumerable canals led into the land like a chequered pattern.

We had no difficulty in crossing the smaller canals, although there was only a single plank as passage. But in our Wanderings through the estate we came to the main canal, which seemed about six to ten yards broad. Across this there was only the usual single plank; and I may confess that I was secretly glad When my wife refused to undertake the crossing! But how were we to get over? Bring some more planks and broaden the pathway? That seemed the obvious plan. But instead, our guide blew a whistle, when there appeared on the other side a workman carrying a long thin pole. He stretched this over, and our guide fitted his end of it to a post with a loop at the top, and the man on the other side did the same. Then I made a great discovery—how easy it is to Walks across any plank, however narrow, if only there is a hand-rail which one can grip.

I took this experience as a parable. We know that the way of duty in life is exceedingly narrow. "Strait is the gate, and narrow is the way." There are times, at deep crossings, when we could gladly call to God to widen the pathway. "It is too narrow, O Lord, I cannot cross." But this is never God's way. The path through temptation and trial is strait and narrow for everyone. It requires courage and bravery to win our way over. But if God will not widen the way, He has graciously given us hand-rails to lead us across—something to which we can hold, and which will steady and keep our feet from falling. You ask me what I mean by these handrails? Well, when I lift up this Bible, that is one. If a man holds on to the truth and teaching of this Book, he will find his pathway made sure and his steps guided over the difficult bits of life. Or I could point you to our Lord Himself. The very knowledge that He is ever present with those who need Him is one of the finest hand-rails a man can have over the crossways and dangers. "Lo, I am with you always, even unto the end." My fellow-soldiers, I know you have difficult experiences and hard temptations to face, more now than ever. God help you to face them! But remember this—there are no experiences you will ever be called upon to bear, no dangers to face, that you may not triumphantly win through, if only you will lay hold of the hand-rails. Your Father knows you need guidance, and He has given it.

The third thing every man needs and desires is a purpose, an aim, an ideal in his life, something to hope and live for. A life without purpose is a life Without result. The men whom we meet in our towns and villages, holding up the street corners and doing nothing except plague themselves and others, are simply the men who from the beginning have had no purpose, no big dream in their life. Without something to live for, the finest talents dribble through our fingers like dry sand; but give me a man, no matter how handicapped in gifts or fortune, who has an ideal and a driving purpose in his heart, and he will do something to the glory of God and man.

Who in all the World has given mankind a hope and a dream like Jesus? I do not speak only of that dream of another life (I wish we spoke less of it), but I speak of His dream for this life. In His own words, "I am come that ye might have life, and that ye might have it more abundantly." My fellow soldiers, if you can tell me of anything that gives your life such a purpose and such a hope, I should like to hear it. Christ will give your days an eternal meaning. He will give you a character, rich and full, that will be your glory. He will bring you to the flower of true manhood. He will lead you into all worthy living. He will train your mind, deepen your sympathies, broaden your outlook, and make you great in His greatness. Surely, you must admit that our Lord Jesus has made human life grand, for He has made it like His own!

Three men in a block-house, chatting with the padre. One of the men remarks, "All I say is, I don't know what good the Church is going to do me!"

I have given you a part of the answer.

A Rose And A Soul

I HAD a talk last week with one of the R.G.A[1]., who complained that the ordinary man in the street does not understand half the terms commonly used in religious conversation. Of course, I didn't hint that part of the fault may lie with the man in the street. This man in the street (what a fabulous creature he is!) does not understand the language of science any more than the language of religion, simply because he has not studied either. The only way to know a thing is to put yourself in the way of knowing it!

Still I believe that this state of things is far more common than we imagine, even among the accepted members of our Churches. There are phrases, laden with all the experience of the saints which are mere sounds to many of our Church members. The particular phrase which my friend mentioned is one that lies right at the base of our religion, and so I make no apology for taking it as the subject of my talk this morning.

We speak about a Christian beginning a "new life" when he accepts Christ. Our Lord Himself spoke about a "new birth." "Ye must be born again," He said. Many people, when they think of this idea, are inclined to ask with Nicodemus, "How can a man be born when he is old?" The whole conception underlying the phrase seems to be quite foreign to their mind. Hence it may not be out of place if I make my talk this morning gather round this sentence, "What do we mean when we speak about a man becoming a new creature in Christ?"

May I ask you to come with me in imagination to a rose-grower's garden sometime in the month of July? Here are innumerable rows of young wild seedling briars, a stock or species which has great vigour and hardiness, but whose flowers, of course, are only the single pink blossoms which decorate our wayside hedge-rows in a wild riot during summer. Let us watch the grower in the interesting work he is now about to undertake. He goes first to his bed of famous exhibition roses, his big, gorgeous "Frau Karl Druschki," his "Juliet," and his "Madame Edouard Herriot." From these and other beautiful roses he cuts out as many "eyes" or "buds" as he may need. Carrying these with him, he goes back to the young wild briars.

---

[1] Royal Garrison of Artillery – a branch of the Royal Artillery

Having cleared away the soil until the base of the briar is exposed, he makes a cut in the young plant as low in the stock and as near the roots as possible. Into this cut he now inserts a trimmed "eye" taken from one of the exhibition varieties. After this the eye is gently tied in with raffia straw, and for the time his operation is complete.

Nature now takes up the running. Gradually the inserted "eye" begins to grow, being absorbed by the parent plant on which it has been fostered. The new shoot which springs from the eye partakes, of course, of the nature of the "Frau Karl Druschki" or the "Juliet" from which it was originally taken. And the gain in the process lies in this, that the grafted shoot grows with the borrowed vigour of the new root on which it is budded, and yet keeps the character and qualities of the old plant from which the "eye" was taken.

But all is not yet done. Once the shoot has fairly started to grow, the gardener goes round and cuts away the other natural shoots of the wild briar, in order to give the more refined rose a chance to grow and prosper. It can now count on a vigorous life, and it in turn begins to send out its own branches, and thus makes the big, strong rose bush which we admire in our garden.

But, even beyond this, another thing is necessary. Unless the gardener takes care, the parent briar will send up sprouting "suckers" from its roots. If these are allowed to grow by neglect, they will soon smother and starve the grafted rose, and the plant will revert back to its wild state.

All this is a parable. If we follow it out, I think it may explain to us some things which appear difficult in the Christian life. If I may say so, we, each one of us, are naturally of the wild briar order. We have plenty of vigour and hardiness, the vigour of our primitive nature; but the flowers we produce, if left to ourselves, are poor and thin and worthless. What can we do, in our own nature, for the glory of God? The best works of men, in themselves, are as poor and thin as the bloom of the wild rose. But Christ, the Gardener, comes to us with a new bud, a bit of His own magnificent nature, and He "inserts" it, puts it into our heart and life. If it "catches on" that is, if we give it a good reception and open our heart, it will begin to grow like the budded eye of the exhibition rose. There is nothing miraculous or against Nature in this, and nothing which may not take place in the life of every man before me. The one thing is, that we should give Christ's Word a chance.

Let us give Him the opportunity of performing this operation in our heart. His life may be budded into us, and will grow and bung forth beautiful flowers to the praise of God.

Why should this thought seem difficult or strange to any of you? Nature is full of examples of this grafting process. I sometimes think the Apostles had thoughts of our gardening operation in their minds. The Apostle James writes "Receive with meekness the engrafted Word, which is able to save your souls." Paul "Thou, being a wild olive, wert grafted in among them, and with them partake of the root and fatness of the olive tree" And do you not think this idea explains that beautiful but difficult passage in the letter to the Galatians: "I live; yet not I, but Christ lives in me: and the life which I now live in the flesh, I live by the faith of the Son of God"?

You ask me what new process occurs when a man becomes a Christian? Does some miracle or some uncanny experience take place in his life? Yes, and No! If we let Him, Christ will come and put a bit of His own nature and spirit into us. He will engraft His Word into our heart. He Will plant His truth, and instil His influence. If We tend and nurture this new bud, it will grow on the wild roots of our nature, and become a plant bearing the blossoms of Christ Himself.

This line of thought leads to many helpful ideas which, if I had time, I should like to develop. But I shall restrict myself to one or two along the line of my parable.

In the first place, like the rose-grower, we must see that the old branches of the briar are ruthlessly cut away. The new life of Christ grafted into us must be given every fair chance to grow and develop. If the other branches are left, or only partially taken away, they will flourish and smother the newly—budded shoot. People sometimes wonder why so many Christians, after an apparently good start, fail and fall short in their spiritual attainments. If I were to venture a reason, I would say it was due to this, that they omitted to prune their life of the habits and desires which formerly possessed them. After a time, when the novelty of their experience wears off, the old practices and passions re-assert themselves, and choke and kill the new shoot. My fellow-soldiers, some of you have lately joined the Communion of our Lord and have professed yourselves His men. The bud has been grafted into you. Christ has put His new spirit and life in your heart. May I say to you, as earnestly as man can, see that you with a firm hand, the old briar: otherwise, in time, they will grow old and smother your new life.

There is only one doctrine for the Christian who would excel, the Doctrine of the Knife. Christ has expressed this truth in that strong but puzzling sentence, "If thine eye offend thee, pluck it out."

Further, remember that, even after this Pruning of the old branches, the wise gardener has to keep his eyes open for the suckers which spring up (sometimes a foot or a yard away) from the briar roots. Need I remind you that there are unsuspected powers and temptations lying dormant in our nature? We hardly know the stuff we are made of ' and it is only trial and time that can show where our weakness lies. Be always on the watch lest the old nature re-asserts itself. If we allow it to sprout out in unsuspected places, it will rob the main plant of its sap and fullness, and in the end, as has often happened, will weaken and kill the good rose.

Now, I have tried to show you, in a parable, what the new life in Christ means, and how it is possible for everyone to receive it. We see that there is nothing astounding in the claim that a Christian may become a "new creature," or may be "born again." He may put on a nature that is new, Christ's own nature. Every man here may experience this joy, if he will only allow the Master Gardener to bud His abounding life into his heart. Let the Word of Christ have an entrance into your minds: give it every chance to develop; clear the ground for its growth. In this, as in everything else, Christianity is all gain. And the difference between your past and your future Will be the difference between the two roses——one thin, weedy and worthless, and the other full, rich and glorious.

May the life of Christ be budded into you!

A Slice In The Wind

MY chief hope at our short evening service is to leave one or two thoughts in your mind which may be of some service in strengthening your hearts and guiding your Ways. Hence, again and again, I have taken a few unconventional subjects; but What does that matter, if only they lead us to some helpful thoughts regarding our spiritual welfare? To-night, of all things, I am going to speak about Golf.

This is the one game I play myself—generally badly. I have observed many of you pitching and putting on the rather rough greens which you have made for yourselves in the field beyond your billets. So I may presume, perhaps, that most of you know the subject as well as I do myself. But in any case, the points I am about to use are so simple and elementary that, even if you do not know the game well, you will have no difficulty in understanding my meaning.

One of the commonest, and at the same time one of the most punishing, faults in golf is what we call the "slice." This occurs by the player failing to swing his club straightly in a sweet circle. On coming to the ball, he cuts across its face, and so gives it a whirling motion which sends it circling off the true course. There is no bad luck about this shot, but only bad play: and generally (though we think differently when we are the sufferers) We deserve all the punishment we get. If the course is properly planned, we shall not only deserve what we get, but we shall also get what we deserve—a bad "lie," rough country, and an awkward approach to the hole. In golf and life alike, the Way of the transgressor is hard!

Now, on a quiet day, when there is little or no wind, a slice may not be badly punished or much off the true line. But do it when the wind is whistling across the course, and see what happens. The ball will swing across the field in half a circle, and, besides leaving you a great distance from the hole, may place you in rough and difficult country.

I have always taken this as a lesson for myself. A slice may be a little fault and may be easily and simply done, but there are circumstances (such as a high wind) which may aggravate it until it becomes the golfer's greatest sin. What does a little fault amount to? Why make a fuss about such a thing as a crusty temper, or an easy carelessness of life, or dourness, or swearing or the thousand little faults about which you preachers are always talking? These are Little things, surely. Why make so much of them? I agree that they may be little things—in a quiet wind! When life is ordinary and easy, when things are normal, when there are no big passions blowing across the course, these little things may not matter much. But then, life is not always sunshine and calm. There are times of great disturbance, when minds are inflamed and passions are quick. That is the day of my fear. You hear, for instance, about a cruel and brutal murder in Edinburgh. How could any man bring himself to do it? He did it, my comrades, in a high wind, when a little fault of hate or envy or greed was magnified into a desperate passion. It is not the little fault I am afraid of; it is the little fault in the high wind.

Jesus our Lord emphasised this point. I am sure the passage in which He refers to it must have occasionally caused you some questioning. Notice His plain words: "Ye have heard that it was said by men of old time, thou shalt not Kill... but I say unto you that whosoever is angry with his brother shall be in danger of the judgment-" Angry with his brother! that is a little thing, surely. Yes, but give that little thing the high wind, and it becomes murder.

Perhaps you now understand the need of attending to little faults. There is nothing "little" in the spiritual life, for anything that may spoil our peace or ruin our life is a power to be reckoned with. Correct your known faults while your life is easy and simple. Who knows when the Day of the High Wind may come?

Again, there is a saying in golf which you must often have heard. When a player is putting for the hole and his ball stops short, his opponent remarks (with feigned sympathy, unless he is a saint!): "Never up, never in." There is reason in this remark; for no matter how accurately and straightly the ball is making for the hole, it cannot possible go down, unless it has sufficient force behind it to carry it right up to the edge. Hence all golfers agree that it is better to be a little beyond the hole with one's putt than a little short of it. In the one case the ball has a chance of going down; in the other it has not.

Life has no more excellent phrase than this one of the golfer: "Never up, never in." Half of our tragedies are made up of people who are not just "up." They are nearly there, nearly fit for their job, nearly fine people, nearly Christians-nearly, but not quite.

"The little more and how much it is;
The little less and what worlds away"

Jesus once gave a striking illustration of this golfer's phrase: "Never up, never in." On one occasion a man questioned Him about God and goodness; and Jesus was so pleased with him and his answers that He made this unexpected reply, "Thou art not far from the Kingdom of Heaven." Not far! Almost Within the line, but just short! In this man's case the remark meant praise. Jesus was astonished to find him so near to the truth He came to preach. But in many another case it is not praise, but blame. "Thou art not far from the Kingdom of Heaven." Nearly up, but not just in! On the borderland, even peeping through the gates! How true this is of thousands of people we know. I have no doubt it is true of some of the men I am addressing. They have a real love for the good life; they admire and revere Jesus; they honour the Church for all it does and represents. But they have stopped a little way short. It is not enough to admire Jesus—can't you love Him? It is not enough to revere Him – can't you give Him your heart? It is not enough to long for goodness – can't you take the one step which, in the love of Jesus, will bring you into touch with it? There are so many men who are nearly right. They are nearly temperate, nearly honest, nearly clean-mouthed, nearly Christian. Thou art not far from the Kingdom of Heaven—but never up, never in.

This one step which is so often wanting represents so much. Our peace and our happiness would be settled if we took it. I should like to think that some man here is now making up his mind to enter into his full kingdom. Take your faith in your hand, and step forward. I have time only to refer to another golfing remark which you will hear on every course in the World. Sometimes, especially with beginners, or even with a good golfer in a slack moment, one may see the player "top" or "duff" his ball, so that the whole force of his stroke is wasted— and sometimes his ball as well! In nine cases out of ten the reason is simple— "Keep your eye on the ball!" Oh, what I have paid in lost strokes and ruined balls for a distracted eye! A man is so keen to watch where he wants his ball to go, that he looks up before the club reaches the ground, and, as a result in his keenness to observe the balls flight, he forgets to observe the ball itself. All good players tell us that the one secret is, "Keep your eye on the ball."

Are we not plagued through life with the distracted eye? The Bible says, "The eyes of a fool are in the ends of the earth," watching every conceivable thing except the one thing that is immediate. I feel sure that the secret of much success is simply concentration. Often the man who climbs to the top is not in any way more gifted or talented than hundreds of others who never succeed. But generally you will find that the successful man is blessed with what others lack—an immense gift of concern ration and application to one particular thing. In business, in politics, in work, he "keeps his eye on the ball." So many of us are dreaming of what we would like to be, that we forget to take the steps to assure that our dream comes true. It is only application to the immediate objects and purposes of life, however lowly and simple these may seem, which will ensure that our ideals are realised.

Is there not a sense in which this phrase applies to Religion? We have one thing to do, and only one – love and serve God. This is literally "man's chief end." And yet how We allow our energies to be distracted so that our concentrated effort is take off our pursuit. I feel more and more that the Christian must learn from the children of the world. A soldier, to be a great soldier, must learn one thing—soldiering. A business man, to be a great power in finance, must learn one thing—business. An artist, to excel in his calling, must apply himself to one thing—art. Is it not true that a Christian, to be a real Christian, must study one thing – Christ? The children of this world are Wise in their generation. Let us imitate their virtues – thoroughness, concentration, a masterly purpose, and ambition. Have we not an ambition, beside which theirs is as nothing? Beware of the distracted eye!

The Worst Military Sin

GREATLY daring, I am going to speak of "things military," and I sincerely hope your superior knowledge may not convict me of "rushing in where angels fear to tread."

What is the Worst military sin? Someone has said that the gravest fault in warfare is to underrate your opponent. It has become an axiom of good general-ship never to despise your enemy. How fatal the sin of underrating may be is seen from some striking instances in history. For example, a hundred thousand Englishmen at Bannockburn laughed at the puny Scottish Army; and yet that little army played with the legions of Edward as the November wind with the autumn leaves. Now, don't let this tickle your Scottish pride! It does not mean that one Scotsman can face two Sassenachs. But it does mean that a host which despises its enemy, and so neglects ordinary precautions, is in danger of a rude blow to its pride.

Or take an instance from our present campaign. If the Kaiser's manifesto regarding our "contemptible little army" is genuine, it forms a modern instance of this ancient sin. For that contemptible little army, standing like a rock, hurled back the German masses and taught them their first and severest lesson.

But while I agree that this sin of undervaluing is unusually serious, I venture to think that there is another more serious. To my mind, it is more serious to overate than to underrate your foe. For, if you think of it, the result of overrating an enemy's power may be the paralysing of all your efforts. If we say "Our foe is too strong and too wonderful; we can do nothing against him," we begin to quake and to give up the fight before it is begun. To regard our opponent as stronger than he really is, to endow him with qualities and powers he does not possess, to believe him invincible and imagine that all our efforts are sure to fail, that is almost certain to paralyse our arm and drain the grit and courage from our heart. If we fight at all, we fight as men who heave stones at the clouds, or as those who wrestle with giants, or as an army, marching to a forlorn hope. It is true that some finely-tempered spirits fight best when they face long odds. But in general, if a man once gets the idea that the weight is against him, his knees become weak: as water, and a possible victory is changed into a sure defeat.

Let me illustrate my view by one or two historical instances. In the time of Isaiah, the little kingdom of Israel lay like a buffer State between the two great world powers of the day—Assyria on the north and Egypt on the south. The politicians of Israel, amateur and professional, were paralysed and hypnotised by the power of these two empires, and being themselves weak in the arm of force, they tried the finger of intrigue. Politicians are seldom men of faith, for inevitably they tend to trust to diplomacy and smartness rather than to honour and God. Hence, with this in view, they tried to play off one Power against the other. But really they were overrating the strength and worth of both empires. what could either of these nations do if God's will was really centred in the future of Israel? And so Isaiah, Walking by faith and not by sight, warned them against overrating the powers of men. "The Egyptians," he cried, "are men and not God, and their horses flesh and not spirit." Only men, and only flesh—nothing more.

In the days of Good Queen Bess, Spain was the ruling Power in Europe. So great was her prestige, and so afraid was England of provoking her wrath, that letters were actually sent to all our mariners warning them against any act which might give a cause of offence to King Philip. The very name of Spain, with her big galleons, hypnotised the mind of England. But a few bright spirits, daring sea-dogs, full of faith in God and England—Hawkins, Drake, and Raleigh—showed that, man to man, an Englishman was the equal 'of a Spaniard. "The Spaniards are men and not God, and their ships are wood and not spirit." And so when the great Armada, with heralded fame and Pope's blessing, came tacking up the English Channel, a few small merchant-ships, rigged out hurriedly as men-of—war, showed this fear-paralysed nation that the Spaniards could be faced and conquered.

When the great Xerxes, King of Persia, who from the day of his accession began to prepare for the invasion of Greece, actually came with his swarming hosts, the Council of the Greek States agreed in despair that it was folly to resist him. What could they do against such an enemy and so they gave up the contest. But Leonidas, the valiant King of Sparta, vowed that, great as the enemy was, he would resist him, though no one else stood by his side. At the historic Pass of Thermopylae, he, with three hundred of his men and a few allies, held the whole Persian host for two days, and in his death taught the hypnotised Greeks that the Persians were only men and not gods. And as a result, at Salamis, the Greeks having plucked up courage swept the Persians back to Asia. 'Now, the Persians are men and not gods, and their horses flesh and not spirit!"

History is full of such instances, if I could take the time to narrate them. Again and again, in face of large odds, small nations have been paralysed by fear. Lunenburg, that choice little duchy, lay down and let the Germans march over it. But, on the other hand, though the contest was almost as hopeless, brave Belgium stood up against the Teutonic hordes, and in her death, as with Leonidas, has taught the world that the Germans are men and not gods, and their horses are flesh and not spirit.

This is a lesson we need to learn. I am convinced that the worst military sin is the crime of overrating. For years Germany has blown her own praises, and, as so often happens with people who talk of themselves, we have taken her at her own estimate. Now that we are in the thick of the contest we have to string up our courage, for we are now realising that, man to man, the Allies are at least her equal.

But there is another warfare, where the same two sins play havoc with our success. On the one hand, many of us underrate what we have to do in the contest of life. A young man generally thinks that he is equal to anything, and as a result he fails to make the needed preparation to face his task. The student slips through his classes as easily as he can; the workman takes his apprenticeship lightly: all of us are somewhat careless in the preparation of our character to meet the trials and difficulties of life. This is one reason why many of us fail. Never underrate what you may have to do. Success of any kind, more so success in character, needs the most careful preparation that we can muster. I implore you, do not treat the problems and tasks of your life too lightly, for this leads to that fatal self-assurance which is one of the big sins of warfare.

But, in spite of this, I believe that the sin of overrating is more serious. May I take two spheres of life and show how this fault may work havoc?

In the first instance, it is ruinous policy to overrate our difficulties. Most of us have these in some measure, but most of us have discovered that with resolution they may be met and overcome. And yet, when we have a task or difficulty to face, how we allow it to paralyse us! It seems so big and looms so large in the dimmest of to-morrow that we hardly know how we can tackle it. Coming troubles cast their shadows before them; and, of course, the shadow is always bigger and darker than the thing itself. Never allow your difficulties to unnerve you! March right up to them with courage, and you will find "their bark is worse than their bite." As with Christian in front of the Palace Beautiful, you will discover that the lions are chained.

But the action of this fault is even more noticeable in another sphere. How we overrate the power of temptation! We know we have an enemy to face. Some of us, by indulgence and by repeated defeats, have strengthened the hands of our foe, until at the thought of our temptations we feel as if we were unable to put up a worthy fight. Many of us are beaten before we strike a blow, for we have given in in

our heart of hearts. This takes the strength from a man's fist and the grit from his heart. He might as well lie down and let the heels of his enemy crush him in the dust, for he believes that his foes are stronger than he—gods and not men, and their horses spirit and not flesh.

We often enter into our temptations with the battle half-lost, having already signed away the victory in our own minds. We look at our temptations through a microscope and see them in huge, ungainly proportions, and the very heart of daring is squeezed out of us. In that moment we forget everything except our own weakness and our enemy's strength; we even forget God and His promise.

Now, in one sense, a man cannot exaggerate too much the power and subtlety of evil. It is a common fault that we are not constantly enough on the alert. Perhaps, as a rule, we enter too easily and unsuspectingly on questionable courses; and we only know that we are snared when we feel the trap spring. But, surely, if by overrating the power of evil We stupefy ourselves in its presence and paralyse our resistance, then to overrate temptation is fatal. The main thing to see not only the forces against us, but also the forces for us, the whole battalions of God and His goodness. And "if God be for us, who can be against us?"

Fellow-soldiers, I have chosen this subject to-day because I know the added temptations of camp life and because I am aware that you can appreciate the military appeal behind my words. Without any doubt your temptations are increased in your present situation, where men are herded together in what is a more or less unnatural life. Your ways are freer and easier; you are away from the quiet restraints of home and civil duty; you find that people make up to you and address you with an unwonted freedom. I should like, therefore, to give you a word of comfort and courage. Remember that there is no situation in life where one may not play the man.

No matter what temptations you may meet, they can be met. Be the Egyptians as strong and fierce as they may, they are men and not gods, and their horses flesh and not spirit. And, what is more, they can be faced as men and conquered by men. It is just devil's doctrine for anyone to think he must go under. The greatest thing that can grip you is not temptation, but the grace of God. Let no enemy, however strong, mesmerise you into weakness.

It all comes to this: Do you believe in the grace of Christ? If you do, when you leave this church turn your face to the enemy with a new light in your eye. Cry out: "I can do all things through Christ who strengthens me." You may forget every word I have said, if you will only remember that sentence. Ring it out again: "I can do all things through Christ who strengthens me." Then in His name and by His strength go forward. Summon up all your manhood to be in league with Christ; shut your teeth like a vice; clench your fingers till they bite into your flesh; but know that in every case you can conquer through Him that loved you. For the Egyptians are only men and not gods, and their horses are only flesh and not spirit.

The Dangers Of The Way

BY his calling every soldier takes his life in his hands. He knows there are dangers through which perhaps he may never come safely. From some chats I have had with officers and men, I gather that almost every soldier is a fatalist He believes—and rightly—that his call will not come before its time. He may not express his ideas in religious terms, but ultimately his point of view amounts to this, "My times are in Thy hand."

Some men, of course, join the colours carelessly, especially at this time, when enlistment is almost an infection. Often it is the khaki, the roll of the drums, the glamour, the adventure, or even the influence of friends or public opinion, which brings us to a decision. But even then a man is not long in the ranks before he grasps the fact that a soldier's life is pre-eminently one of possible danger. The long lists of casualties, which strike on our hearts like daily blows, soon convince us that We must be willing to face "the ultimate chance." Once we are sent to the front, who knows how many of our gallant lads will ever come home?

I should not be a faithful chaplain if I did not give you something to think of, in view of the evident dangers of your calling. I have spoken to you at other times of the comfort and hope of our faith, a faith which will lead us to count duty above danger, and honour above fear; but to-day I should like to confine my talk to the thought of the dangers you may have to encounter. After all, the best way to conquer fear is to look it in the face.

There is a text in the 91st Psalm which runs thus: "Thou shalt tread upon the lion and adder: the young lion and the dragon shalt thou trample under feet." This verse occurs in a real soldier's psalm. From the beginning to the end it is concerned with the dangers of life. Notice the military phrases scattered through it: "My refuge and my fortress;" "Thy shield and thy buckler;" "The arrow that flies by day;" "A thousand shall fall at thy side." Take this psalm and make it your own : it was written for soldiers!

The verse I have chosen speaks of three types of danger under the guise of three animals, and exhibits God's promise of safety against all three.

The first of these is the Lion. Round the thickets and jungle of

Jordan the lion had his lair. His roar was the terror of the night, and as he crept forth at twilight, hungry for his prey, his cry chilled the hearts of the shepherds watching on the hillside, or silenced for a moment the evening gambols of the children in the village huts. Lord of the night! king of the jungle! It was better to be safe behind lock and key when his majesty took his stroll, praying meanwhile that the belated traveller and the unfended[2] cattle might escape his royal notice.

The next was the Adder, lurking in the tangled grass. As the labourer trudged homeward through the undergrowth of the jungle, as the reaper cut the ripe corn with his rude hand sickle, as the children gathered tomorrow's faggots[3] in the neighbouring wood, who could say when the adder might spring, with that warning hiss that usually came too late?

The third was the Dragon, that beast as imaginary as the elves and bogies with which we often give "pleasant shivers" to our little children. The Jewish people believed in the monstrous dragon as surely as our young ones believe in Father Christmas, or the fairies and goblins of Hans Andersen. What a crushing, paralysing belief this must have been! The giant Leviathan, the demons of the air, Azazel of the desert, the Baalim who dwelt in the groves! Can you realise how the minds of these people must have been possessed by the fear of these wicked spirits, who delighted to tantalise men? That, by the way, is the great need of missionary enterprise in our Churches, to save our ignorant savage brethren from cruel fears like these.

These are the three animals against whose power the psalmist is promised security. Of course, by the civilised state of our land and by the growth of education, we are secure from the fear of all three. But are we secure from the very real dangers of which they are but a type? I believe, fellow-soldiers, that there is still room for this old promise in your lives.

For, in the first place, the lion evidently is only a type of life's open, fierce danger which comes at us in plain combat. It represents the horror which straddles across our path and dares us to battle, which roars out its defiance, and which can only be met by pluck, endurance, and faith. What life has not its measure of this danger? Even as civilians, we knew that we had to count on this. There are occasions in every walk of life

---

[2] Unfended – from fend (to look after) unfended – not looked after

[3] Faggots - a bundle of sticks or twigs bound together as fuel

which can only be faced with such bravery as you would tackle a lion in the way, difficulties which can only be encountered with a blow from the shoulder, sorrows you have just to win through with tight lips, problems into which you must flounder straight ahead with a prayer in your heart, temptations at which you have to lunge with sword and bayonet. There they are before you – agonising duties, problems, and responsibilities. Up and at them, in God's strength: it's the only way! Face the lion and pluck it by the beard. God and a resolute heart can win through anything.

If that is true of civilian life, how much more true it is of the military life you now lead. Think of our soldiers in France and the Dardanelles, and our fine lads on the sea. They know there is fierce danger before them. But they know that the only way is the manly Way, to face it. The reins of your life are in God's hands. I like your soldier's fatalism, only I should like it to be faith instead of fatalism. Take this sentence as a motto: "A man is immortal till his work is done." Thou shalt tread upon the lion!

In the same way, the adder that lurks in the long grass may symbolise something very definite in our modern life. Does it not suggest the hidden dangers of the world which spring upon us at our unwary moment, the worn link we had not noticed, the weakness we had not suspected, the trouble we had not anticipated, the temptation we had not feared? As the labourer strolls along the path the adder nips him from the grass. It looked a sunny meadow, but there was subtle danger. I speak in a parable— the plank that looked strong, the ice that seemed firm, the sword in the velvet, the treacherous bog, the deed that seemed innocent, the friend who appeared loyal! Do these not suggest to us the dangers of the unwary moment?

You can hardly guess what may meet you in the near future. You are now in the hands of our military authorities, and you may be moved anywhere within a few hours' notice. But I can tell you one thing sure amid the things that are uncertain— wherever you go, and however you are assailed, you can take your God with you. Nothing can happen to snatch you out of His hands. There is no temptation and no danger for which he will not give you the needed strength. "He that dwells in the secret place of the Most High shall abide under the shadow of the Almighty. I will say of the Lord, He is my refuge and my fortress: my God: in Him will I trust." Thou shalt tread upon the adder!

But what of the dragon, that torment of the Jewish mind? Did you ever see a dragon? Have you ever talked with a fairy or chatted with a goblin? Why, in the school-boy's phrase, "there ain't no dragon!" That is just the point—there never was, and there never will be, such a fabulous creature. The dragon was the weird invention of childish tribes, who feared the unknown and peopled the darkness with the creatures of their own imagination. It represents the old sin of invented danger, godless worry. Are there not thousands of people whose peace of mind is broken by the foolish dangers they invent?

Yet our invented dangers and our worry may be very real. I was speaking with a sergeant the other day who made this remark: "I don't care so very much what happens to myself, but I can't keep my thoughts off my wife and my little boy." I know there are many of you who already, in your own mind, have dedicated your lives to the service of your country; and yet the danger you fear is not What may happen to you, but to those who are dependent on you. Everyone of us can sympathise with the anxieties of a good father or a dutiful son. Such thoughts only do you honour. But, surely, if you can trust yourself in the hands of God, you can trust your loved ones also. He who keeps you will keep your jewels.

As we look to the future our hearts are concerned with what it may hold for us. If that be so, let us, like this psalmist, look first to the past. He built his confidence for to-morrow on God's goodness yesterday can we, too, not acknowledge that every hour of our lives we have been kept and guided? There were some temptations that seemed heavier than we could bear, some griefs that seemed too deep for tears. And yet, when We came to the sea, a way, a perfect wall of waves, was opened for us right through the depths and we came dry-shod to the other side. If so from that past experience, look now to the future. Circumstances may differ, but God is the same. Remember, He offers us no promise of an easy road, no promise of continual sunshine, no promise that the beasts of the jungle will not molest us. We may not be free from struggle, on or temptation, or sorrow, or death. But none of these shall triumph over us — even in death, we are victors.

"Thou shalt tread upon the Lion, and the Adder, and the Dragon."

Get To Your Marks!

I HAD the pleasure of being a judge at your sports yesterday at Dalmeny. It reminded me of the days when I thought myself a sprinter, when in fact I neglected my school studies for all sorts of field pastimes, and incidentally brought down on my head an elder brother's sarcastic remark: "Well, old man, if you can't win prizes with your head, you can win them with your feet!"

But yesterday's sports brought me not only memories, but 'also reflections. I began to remember how the Apostle Paul used to enforce his talks by homely illustrations from the famous Greek and Roman games of his day. Again and again We find him referring to the trained athlete, and wishing that, in the race of life, men would prepare themselves as thoroughly as they do for their sports. For, after all, life is a race, with a course to run, with laws for training, with conditions for entrance, and with prizes for heroism and endurance. But what a race it is, and how many fail! It is run through the years, and needs constant steady going. As with the distance events yesterday, some start off with a rush and seem to have the prize already in their hands. But here, as always, it is training, skill, a stout heart, and conserved energy that tell. How often shall the last be first and the first last! In the light of these sports there is no word in the Bible that is more eloquent than this: "He that endures unto the end shall be saved."

There is one special reference of the Apostle to the famous Greek games to which I should like to ask your attention to-day. Writing to Timothy, his young disciple, he says in his letter: "And if a man also strive for the masteries, yet is he not crowned, except he strives according to the rules." That means, obviously, that if a man is ready to run in the sports, he cannot receive the prize unless he is willing to obey the rules of the game. Our British sense of fairness agrees that this is right. As one of your judges, I should have disqualified any man who did not run fairly, and I believe that your common idea of justice would have supported me in my ruling.

Now that our thoughts are still on the events of yesterday, I should like to use the opportunity to speak to you about the three great rules which governed the Greek games, and, if possible, apply them afterwards to the greater Christian race.

The first of these I might call the Law of the Age Limit. In certain of the large games, and especially in the important events, it was made a strict rule that only men between certain ages were eligible to compete. The intention of this rule is quite plain. On the one hand, it would have spoiled the interest of the contest if raw, unformed, flabby boys were allowed to enter. However keen they were, as the pace was punishing, it would have been foolish to allow callow youths to contend with strong picked men; and, on the other hand, it would have been as foolish, for the interest of the sport, to allow men to enter who were past their best and had grown stiff and soft. It was the purpose of the games that picked men from all parts, in the very "pink" of form, should strive and contend under equal conditions. Not only was this fair, but it also assured that the sports would be grandly contested and the interest kept keen to the finish.

Is there such a law as this in the race of life, the law of the age limit? Without any doubt, it works in every sphere of endeavour. The man who begins to study in middle life, for instance, cannot hope, other things being equal, to cope with those who have had a start of years. He may do wonders, but he will never do all he might have done. It may be only the more honour that he should start at this late hour. But that is not my point: he can never make up for the lost years! Remember this, as time and opportunity slip through the easy grasp of youth: "Redeem the time."

But there is a more pressing aspect of this thought. Is this law of the age limit true of the Christian life? Is there an age limit beyond which a man cannot hope to grasp the prize of God? I should be foolish to say so. That robber, hanging by the side of Christ, would rebuke me, for he found paradise and death in the same hour. I thank God there is no time too late for anyone to know and serve their Lord. There have been men who have found the prize of Christ when every other prize in life was already beyond their reach. This is the glory of the Gospel—that literally, while there is life, there is hope.

But even in this matter there is another side as true. We are familiar with the old saying that few men are converted after forty. Youth is the plastic period, and after a certain age a hardening process sets in, and We become so grooved in our ways that We are difficult to move. That is one fact; and another is this, that if, as we believe, the Christian gain is character, rich, deep and tested, then it stands to reason that no late-comer to Christ can ever be as finely sifted and tested as he might have been, had he had years of Christian character behind him. If there is any true growth and development in the Christian life, then it is only time and experience that can give them. That is why I am so urgent with you now, my comrades. The race for the Prize of Christian character is a long and unending pursuit. It is common sense to begin when you are fittest, when your body is at its best, your mind impressionable, and your sympathy easily moulded. Remember the law of the age limit! If you Wish the highest results, begin the race while your wind is good and your heart is stout.

The second law in the famous games was the Law of Training. A man might be Within the prescribed ages, but in addition to that he had to take an oath before the altar of Zeus that he had spent at least ten months in preparation for the games. Some authorities also say that the competitor had to undergo thirty days' special practice at Elis before coming to the Stadium. We can easily understand the value of this regulation. The races were hard and testing, and untrained men Were sure to drop out and so lessen the interest of the struggle. This stringent law of training, therefore, was made binding on all in order that the sport might be of the finest rank.

Who would deny that the law of training applies to the race of life? Genius may lift a man high, but unless genius itself is trained and educated it will miss the crown. You yourselves as soldiers are the best proof of training. When I meet any of you in the street or pass you on sentry duty, I can generally tell whether you are a trained man or a raw recruit. For in soldiering, as in life, training tells. Extend this thought outwards, and you will see the need of training for the Christian. As we make the muscle of our arm strong, so we should strengthen the fibre of our character. A man cannot win the crown in the Christian life unless he brings himself to his fittest. Keep your minds open and your hearts responsive to the truth of God, and above all train yourselves in His Word. What is there more pathetic than a man of flabby character and weak life?

The third great law was the Law of Fair Running. Once the men are trained and on their marks, there comes the race itself. Unfortunately, there are "crooks" here as everywhere. There is, for instance, the man who tries to sneak a yard; the man who believes in beating the pistol; and the man who, if he cannot oust his opponents fairly, will do it foully. Oh, I know the dodges, both by the runners and the spectators. "I shall never forget, after I had won my heat" in some big sports at Glasgow, how a weed of a "bookie" came up and asked me, "What will you take to lose your next heat?" I nearly told him what I would take to kick him out of the field! Or I think just now of one of my friends who was running on the same field and was slashed down the leg by the spikes of the man he was passing at the far end of the course. Well did the Greeks say that no man could win the prize unless he ran according to the rules.

The law of fair running I does that apply in life? Thank God, it does, in the long run. We have an old Scotch phrase "Cheatery chokes," and it is true! In the best sense, and indeed in the only sense, evil never prospers. I don't like the method of expressing, but I like the thought, in the old proverb "Honesty is the best policy." Whatever you are hoping to do or become, fellow soldiers, seek it honestly and honourably. Foul means never led to a fair end. Seek to live your life, do your business, and find your recreation in the spirit of Jesus. Do you remember that our Lord was once tempted to take the low road to the high end? When He spent that season of agony in the desert, undergoing His temptation, you remember how evil suggested to Him that He might win the world in an easy way. "All these things will I give thee, all the kingdoms of the world and the glory of them" (and that was what Christ sought), "if thou wilt fall down and worship me." But Christ could do His work only in His own true way and spirit. One cannot do God's work without God's tools.

The sports of yesterday are past, but life is an unending race. It may be a long time before some of us are asked to "breast the tape"; others, if We are sent to the front, may reach the goal the sooner. But there is one curious thing regarding the Christian race which I should like you to know—a man may win the crown before he breasts the tape. It is Christ who gives the prize, but it is Christ who is Himself the prize. He who has Christ in his heart is already victor, for he has gained even now all that God could give him—Life and its Lord.

Get to your marks, then! This is the day of opportunity.

Come Out And Stay Out

If I were to use a lively phrase, I should say that the secret of the Christian life is, "Come out and stay out." The one implies that we should take a clear stand on the important things of life, and the other that, having taken it, we should keep it. On the Whole, I believe the first is easier than the second. Most people are open to some impression, and there are times in every life when we are moved by the appeal of truth or emotion. Under the influence of this it is not difficult to turn our backs on folly or seek wisdom. The real difficulty lies in "staying out," once we have "come out." There are so many things which begin to tell on our state of mind. For one thing, the original emotion begins to wear thin: time itself alters the appeal of a bygone decision; we begin to settle down again into our ordinary Ways, and we are apt to slip back, almost unconsciously, into our old habits. Undoubtedly it is harder to "stay out"!

For instance, a young lad, under enthusiasm for his country, enlists as a gunner or a sapper in one of your companies. At the beginning, because his keenness is still strong and the novelty is undimmed, he is as "hot as mustard." But give him eight or nine months of duty at the guns, without any of the excitement of battle (as has been the case with many here), and you will find what his original keenness was worth. I know that those who have been at duty since War was declared will appreciate my point.

Carry this over into our religious life, and I have a tale which may interest some of you. How many of those who hear me have joined the Church since war began? I am glad to think that under the work of the various chaplains some hundreds of your companions have taken this step. In line with my phrase, you have "come out." You have come out from the indifference and carelessness of the world, and have taken your stand by the side of Christ. You have "enlisted," as surely as you enlisted for King George.

But while I rejoice at your decision, I am far more anxious that you should keep true to it. The hardest bit of the road is before you. Anyone, under the big moving ideas of this war, may have his mind and heart stirred in unsuspected ways. Thousands all over the country have been so touched that they have been led into a new relation to God and God's Church. But the main thing is that, having come out, you and those like you should stay out. There will be countless temptations for you to face. You may have to endure the jeering of companions; your own early emotion may fade; you may be placed in situations which may try your faith and resolution. This will be your test. Be loyal, at all costs, to your vows. Strengthen your spiritual life day by day. There is no reason why each one of you should not prove a worthy helper in Christ's Kingdom, a real soldier of the Cross.

Meanwhile, in view of this rough bit of the road which lies before you, I should like to say something to you about taking your stand, or, as I have called it, "coming out and staying out." In order to do this, may I select as my subject an incident in the Early Church which was very similar to your experience?

There were some men in Ephesus who had made their living by selling amulets and charms and scrolls to the superstitious worshippers of the Ephesian goddess. you know what I mean—-the charm which is supposed to bring good luck, or the scroll with fancy writing on it which is believed to ward off evil. The Ephesian people, in their folly, paid big prices for these things; and of course it was a very lucrative business for the traders. We soldiers need not smile at the gullibility of these people: have we not our battalion mascots, which are believed to be lucky? The other day there were four of us sitting together, and one of the company handed round cigarettes. Striking a match, he lit two, and then blew the match out. Why? Oh, I see you smiling! You all know the reason, for almost every soldier I meet believes that it is unlucky to light three cigarettes with one match!

Well, the people of Ephesus were as superstitious as soldiers—or sailors. And the sellers of charms made great profits. Into this city came Paul, preaching the love and goodness of God in Jesus. I am glad to say that many believed, among them some of these men who traded with scrolls and charms on the people's credulity. They, "came out." Notice their conduct, for in it lies the secret of "staying out."

We read that they brought all their scrolls and charms and amulets, and burned them in a public place[4], to show that they were done with evil and superstition forever.

This suggests to me three secrets of "staying out."

[4] Acts 19:19

I. Burn your books, and so break with the past. These men gave up everything that held them to their old trade. This is our safety also. It is pitiable to see a man tugged between two allegiances—his heart divided between two kingdoms and his will weakened between two affections. It is a clean-cut cleavage we need. I may liken our connection with the past to a rope. Most of us, when We join cause with Christ, take the knife and make an honest slash at the rope. But unfortunately, the tie that holds us to the past is strong, and it calls for many a thrust. Some of us do manage to break it, but most leave some few strands un-severed. And We say, "What do these few frayed strands matter?" But I have seen these slim threads draw a man slowly but surely back to the old life of sin. Men, in this thing there is only one way. Cut the rope! Burn the books! Close the door!

2. Let your companions know what you stand for. The men at Ephesus chose the most public place for their bonfire, in order that all people might understand that they were now done with their past life. This was Wise, for I am sure that half our temptations overtake us because others do not know what we represent. The undecided man is always a mark for trial. For instance, if a soldier is known among his companions as an abstainer, it stands to reason that he is not pestered with half the foolish invitations to drink which play havoc with the ordinary man. If people know that we are decided on any matter, we are saved from irritating suggestions. That is the great value of a public stand such as you have taken in joining the Church. You are showing your colours.

In a busy city in America the magistrates and people were constantly annoyed at the untidiness of the streets. They believed that their squad of scavengers was sufficient for the work, but somehow the work was not done. One genius in the council suggested an expedient which effectually solved the difficulty. He proposed that every scavenger should be supplied with a white jacket. The idea looked foolish, but it worked, for now every street-cleaner was a marked man. People who had passed him unnoticed before saw him now and observed if he were idle. It is said that the streets of that city were never so clean.

I believe that a public stand is a great help to a man's resolution. Generally, I do not believe much in "pledges." But, on the other hand, if a crutch helps a poor beggar to walk, who am I that I should despise his crutch? I certainly believe that all of us would be stronger and less tempted if the world, by our public profession, knew what we stood for. Put on the white jacket!

3. Be ready to pay your price. Everything in life has to be paid for in some way or other. If we join Christ and undertake to follow Him, we shall have to sacrifice something. Mark you, I do not believe that a man loses anything worth having when he throws in his lot with God. Religion is all gain—gain in strength, happiness manliness, and true life. But some things we may like, which are yet evil, may have to go by the board. These people in Ephesus did not only burn their books, but also their livelihood, they had to give up their trade and start looking for some new line of life more honourable. This is the test of a man's sincerity. But it is also one secret of his future strength.

You have "come out"; and the problem is, how can you "stay out"? How can you keep the new life you have begun strong and even stronger as the days go by? The one big secret, of course, is to live daily in the love of Christ. Today I give you three smaller secrets. Though they are less than the greatest, do not despise them:

- Burn your books!
- Put on the White jacket!
- Pay the price!

Also by James Black - The Mystery of Preaching

Apart from this excellent book Around the Guns – James Black also wrote several other works that are also well worth reading.

I first came across the Mystery of Preaching on a recommended reading list back in 1992 from a preacher in my local church. It was to be several years before I found my own copy. Once opened I found Dr Black's rhetorical style and content to be refreshing and informative.

Dr Black brought a sense of Godly conviction on the subject of honouring the preached word and a new challenge on expectations of what the word will produce.

I would urge any Christian who wants to take preaching seriously to read and absorb Dr Black's words.

This Heritage reprint is of Dr Black's original 1924 edition.

ISBN: 978-1-910372-07-4 Paperback
ISBN: 978-1-910372-08-1 Paperback
ISBN 978-1-910372-09-8 Kindle/Kobo

Sharif George
Parvus Magna Press

Also Published by Parvus Magna Press

Foundations of Faith for New Believers – Leaders Manual

Foundations of Faith for new believers is a series of 10 Bible Studies around the basics of the Christian faith. The 10 subjects including Faith, Salvation and Prayer are easy to understand simple Bible studies that encourage the new Christian in their faith and encourage them to ask questions about their walk with God.

The Foundations of Faith series has sold over 30,000 copies since it was first published about 15 years ago and has helped thousands of new believers become valuable members of the congregation.

This is the Leaders Manual which has plenty of space for notes and comments for the study leader and you can also get a student's manual.

Paperback ISBN 978-1910372005

Kindle ISBN 978-1-910372-06-7

Foundations of Faith for New Believers – Students Manual

This is the Student Manual which is a great give-away, either at the start of the course or at the end as a prize for further study. All of the material contained in the leader's manual is here for the students.

Paperback ISBN 978-1910372012

www.ingramcontent.com/pod-product-compliance
Lightning Source LLC
Chambersburg PA
CBHW081547040426
42448CB00015B/3246